dying in the scarecrow's arms

Also by Mitchell L. H. Douglas

Cooling Board: A Long-Playing Poem
blak\ *al-fə bet*\

dying
in the
scarecrow's
arms

Poems
Mitchell L. H. Douglas

A Karen & Michael Braziller Book
PERSEA BOOKS / NEW YORK

Persea Books, Inc.
277 Broadway
New York, New York 10007

LCCN: 2017959223

Book design and composition by Rita Lascaro
Typeset in Simoncini Garamond
Manufactured in the United States of America
Printed on acid-free paper

Acknowledgments

Thanks to the editors of the following journals and anthologies where some of the poems in this volume first appeared (sometimes in slightly different versions):

African Voices: "After murder," and "O-H-I-O" (published as "Your welcome")

Black Bone: 25 Years of the Affrilachian Poets: "127 Notebooks" and "Is it wrong"

Blood Lotus: "The Illusion of Hips" and "Persist (I)" (published as "She Plants the First Kiss")

Indianapolis Review: "Haints"

Kinfolks Quarterly: "Two Black writers walk into a bar in Colorado is not the beginning of a racist joke"

Not Like the Rest of Us: An Anthology of Contemporary Indiana Writers: "Continuum" (published as "After days of murder, more bodies")

Poetic Voices Without Borders: "False Starts for Cursed Letters"

Resisting Arrest: poems to stretch the sky: "Blood Aubade, 1969"

Small Batch: An Anthology of Bourbon Poetry: "Day one"

Washington Square Review: "Circle"

Contents

cross frame

spark, earth

Ení, a character created for this volume, is a heroic figure presented with the intent of capturing fragments of an endless epic. Pronounced "any," it is Yoruba for "one."

like
putting a match in my mouth
and striking the cigarette—
                    —Etheridge Knight

dying in the scarecrow's arms

Loosies

Right now, I shouldn't be
the cigarette dangling

from the mouth of the man
you will ride

like a Derby horse
to roses. His name:

Eric. Your bloodline:
Pantaleo.

          Fuck
persona, calculated

throat clutch, note control. How
can I mimic & sing

through scream?
        For you, this is fantasy: the pony

you've always wanted, a story
to share in the squad room

when the day is done & men
of power fall into territorial pissing.

       Yes, he is bigger. Are you
frightened? Yes,

he is a man. Does the mass
make him less?

      Is the story spinning
your gears, do you dream

of besting the thin blue
w/the one that didn't get away?

      This is sport to you,
the choke, grip

& spin. No applause,
but you hold on,

count seconds
like cowboys do.

      Cigarettes was it?

      I think I know the way

this works, the hope
& crash.

          Just
bear witness, say

the words: A man w/a wife
& kids is dead

over loosies, & suddenly
the centuries—

17th & 21st—have burns
to share.

cross frame

Used. Sold.

For Mitchell,
Thank you for rescuing this book
    —Martín Espada, April 27, 2007
        (inscription in City of Coughing and Dead Radiators,
        removed from circulation, Rochester Hills Public Library,
        Rochester, Michigan)

There is no easy way to explain this,
but there was a time when you
were unwanted & you wound up
here.
        Or
w/litte space for extra, someone
thought about what they could do
w/out, plot & POV, & you
wound up here.
        Or
after a question of worth, how much
for this or that, tercet & foot, & you
were thought to be something
of value, but not
enough to keep.

There's really no nice way
to say *This*
is not your home, but you are
here, & what's that like,
standing in place
night after night,
your spine exposed?

Circle

and the road twisted on to his loveless house
and his cornfield dying
in the scarecrow's arms.
        —Robert Hayden

Today the sun
has fists, not rays. Nothing delicate
happens here. Watch
the beating that goes
ignored: The Circle, evening,
the monument in call
of war, a common Indiana
ranch w/the roof
ripped off.
                Boruch says the Midwest is sieve, pass-
through, permanently
in transit, flux.
It is the get-here-to-get-there,
the sun's mapped fists
in an orange 6 o'clock
beat down, the tenants
strewn about the concrete circumference, liquid
in states of rest, skin & bone
poured over the curb
of South Meridian, splayed
beneath a mailbox, propped against
a garbage can outside
St___b___s. The suits'
& walkers' heads turn,
sidestepping the future
they escaped, eyes on
a latte, the next block.
        Today the sun
has a better haymaker,
a better uppercut,
a wicked right/left combo.
Today the sun
is perfecting its roundhouse,

& his size 14 keeps connecting
left jaw, right jaw, you would cry,
but there's no layaway
for tears. So you cuddle up
on an asphalt couch
next to your brothers & sisters,
the Styrofoam maracas
of cups & change lulling you to rest
like the pluck
of kalimbas in turning
signals, the basslines
car horns hang
in exhaust
cruising through your living room
on an airless city night.

After murder,

        the complex changes
names. The Flats,
The Villas, pretty gauze
for old wounds. As if

we forgot the bullets,
the children that fell, the angry
boyfriends living w/children
they do not love. I drive by
& try to remember when

pieces fit. A cloud
of cardinals explodes
from a snow drift, the splash
of my tires etching dirt

in the bank. All this flying,
impact, stain. Don't tell me
you can't see.

False Starts for Cursed Letters

@ the grocery,
found a losing lottery ticket
@ the bottom of my basket,
a bad luck sign
if I ever saw one . . .

†

I am
the bite from your morning
apple, skin removed, pulp
browning in air.

†

Can I be something other
than pieces?

†

Bed unmade for two days,
better this way I tell myself.
Tried to burn your number,
but flame won't make it fade . . .

†

I am
the mark that wraps your finger,
skin's record of days, reminder
of the ring, removed.

†

Can I be something
other than missing?

Two Black writers walk into a bar in Colorado is not the beginning of a racist joke

it is us   the sinew   marrow & caw   the way we twist words like arms
behind backs   howl @ the puzzle   We belly up to the bar   dare a
motherfucker to say something about Alizé or Courvoisier   Red wine
& bourbon working spells   we conjure the Black Canon   our textual
constellation   (Toni & Langston)   politic   on whether there is space
for us   We ignore ski lodge décor   ESPN   the wigged woman w/
clothes too thin for November   her disappearing act to the elevator   the
reappearance minutes after   (silent & disheveled)   No we don't   Notice
is what we do   our lives devoted to lines of witness   Your missed flight
my arrival   the bartender ogling the emerald glow of your dress   the ink
that snakes my arms   every eye   on guard

Day one,

I sip the shoulders
off a bottle of oak—
some new wild

that turns my head—
& all I dream is you:
the confirmation of failure

I hope to run into,
prowling each plastic dive
in this blue horse town.

The haves & have nots
@ barn's length, money
ever thinner,

      many a night spent
drunk w/the thought
of you, sheet wind,

pillow cool. Oh
the reach
of your hand, cast

of sun & dusk. This first
step of fall—everything
undone & wanting—

a rick I stack alone.

{Ení (in Therapy)}

I have become rather fond
of setting things on fire
& walking away. My therapist
calls it abandonment;
I call it boredom.
          I fired my therapist,
but on my first day home, back
to the house of the timid, I burned
four pieces of bacon before giving
up, settling on cereal.
                              There was no hunger,

just the thought that wouldn't more
be nice. Why not have more?
My therapist calls it boredom. I call her
          widow.

The Illusion of Hips

after Lucille Clifton

Caught in the angle of sun & slight breeze, her skirt, melon, balloons. *This,* she says, *is for the illusion of hips,* but she needs nothing to make her more. Petal & stem, hair like a crown of baby's breath falling to her shoulders, sweet rain. Born in Buffalo, she studied @ the same high school as Ms. Lucille, which tells me she could be a poet by osmosis, a good one even (something in the water). Please forgive me, I am trying to describe beauty, inner & outer, & isn't that always the trouble: the risk of walking in stale words? I am trying not to be that poet, I am trying to impart honor, & I will be successful when I mention that after talking about the hips she doesn't have, she smiles like a new world, & you nod your head   know exactly what I mean.

Ekphrasis: Giza '61

Perhaps it's not the way
Satchmo's horn is an angle
of light—the bell
raised to heaven—or

the way Lucille smiles
her approval, leans back
into the space
meant for music. Notice

the pyramids, the Sphinx
in the ancient distance,
& thanks to the illusion
of the capture, its stone lips

seem poised to kiss
Louie's hands, a blessing
of the highest calling. Yes,
love can be measured

breath, a divining
rod w/valve & gleam,
(around Lucille's neck, binoculars?)
a note to sift the sand.

Selma Love Song

Like Son's sweet resonator,
I am the honey bee moan
in your tender ear:
silver howl, cross-

road breath. This body
tuned & flawed,
the fretboard
a plank of mercy.

In the burn
of the baddest juke,
no soul fears dance,
damns touch. Our hands,

dear God, sign
the wanting. They tremble,
slide   release
the loudest chords.

Why Grits Burn So Bad

               As I make a late breakfast,
my 8-year-old cheers

@ the promise of grits. Surely
there is a little Southern woman

in her soul. You wonder
how grits could ever

be a weapon, flung
hard from the hand

of a lover scorned, the way
the grains wrap & cling, refuse

to be lonely. All that flesh she loved
burning now, past simmer, full

on boil. I can only feel sorry
for the Reverend, any note

he ever sang pale
in the company

of hot warble. I spoon
a healthy portion

on my daughter's plate
& shiver. If

you reached the end of this poem
& all you can say is, "Shouldn't it be

'Badly,' not 'Bad'?"
               I bet
you've never been loved.

{Ení (Woke up Sunday Saturday night drunk)}

                                    late for a flight & unpacked. We poets close
bars: flash ID for IPA, flirt w/the cropped crown waitress (soft eyes, bare
shoulders, tats). Glass after glass until her eyes go steel, point us to the
door.

                            It's 3 a.m.

Three days in DC & I am window, NW damp beneath overcast, clouds
tossing holy water while I pray for stained glass corners. We walk streets
like church aisles, my blood: communion wine. Walk like the answer is on
the next corner. No, after that, after ... The father, son, & leaden spirit.
More steps toward understanding ... Lord, deliver us. & by us, I mean ...

Persist

I.
She plants the first kiss
in the back of a taxi, cabbie
craning his neck, eyes in rearview
to catch the warm press of lips.
                    We run
from cab to night, capital
breath pinning us to the hip
of One Way & DON'T
WALK, signs blinking black
surrender as we stand
in more eyes, the whip
of wind,
            kiss again. Ready

for knees, the kneel
& spin of our steal-
away song, I stop her
in winter's thaw, chirp
        I love you
before feet rush
our bodies indoors
to corner tables
& candlelight.
        Yes,
        you do
she laughs, & I
lose my coat,
get acquainted
w/cold.

Oak

After a night of indulgence, your snifter
filled to the hips w/sweet brown clear,
leave a taste @ the foot, rest
your head & dream of other rich nights.
In the morning, if your head is steady, stomach
ready for the day's first meal, check

that glass again. The clear brown
is now cloud, resin
of the barrel. W/care, raise the glass
to your nose, inhale the memory. But never—no
never—taste. That time, dear one,
is all but ash.

The Poem that Makes You Love Me

Forgive
      my belly
      taut
w/wish.

Heretics

Neighbors say leaves fell,
but they never gathered, they
being those who came before us,
let this yard
go to hell.
                    What to say to the family
that brings this blight (see
line five)? Our backyard
the part of the park
you warn your kids
to stay away from: bare
patches of dirt, crabgrass,
a few blades, sparse
above the surface, a broken
glass (from the house?), a beer bottle
from God knows when,
& the branches, so many,
brittle against the sun, the yard
a kind of kindling.

                    All @ once you say
this poem is too bourgeois,
the concern of a lawn, a backyard ...
I am your audience, & I
live in a basement apartment,
not a tree in sight, wish
I had a space w/grass missing
to complain about. & if
this poem is to be called heretics,
perhaps the rebellion you speak of
is a poet rejecting the language of poetry,
the rules we know, not the previous
tenant who took such ill care
of the property. & to that, I cannot
quarrel, add this: sometimes
the best efforts end in failure, the point

abandoned like broken
branches, so many
falling leaves.

Blood Aubade, 1969

for Fred Hampton & Mark Clark

Chairman's head
swims a dream, lover
& unborn son: his crown, wing.

                                How heavy the body
in sleep/death, drag
to vacant doorway, head
a woolen quill, scrawls black
blood @ the hooves of "men."

                        Was it by arm, a fist-
full of hair, yank from the rouge
of the pierced bedroom?
If you know a bullet's wrath—wood splinter,

plaster   )blast(steel drum tap
dance, box spring (catch all) humming
like a hive of bees—you know
the gauge.
In the fury—shots
first, no questions, pigs
(black & white) squeal
@ 4:30 a.m.   false aubade.

The bed:
soft alter,
no offer
to our gods.

(In Medias) Res

. . . that stops before my house each morning, the one the man who drives the white pickup with no door to protect the bed depends on. Somehow, they let him ride w/out pay, his tool belt enough for the price of admission. But me: A messenger bag says nothing or everything @ once. One failing testimony: A man w/a messenger bag has the coin to catch a ride. Pay up. I do & find a seat in the front. Out of spite, I tell all the white men that they will be giving up their seats to black women today: young, old, w/or w/out child—no excuses. Your seat, sir. Then I laugh, retract the sir, replace it w/"your wackness," & now everybody is confused. "I believe that relates to Hip-Hop, but his use of the messenger bag points to a more professional Negro who would know nothing of that music," says the freeloader w/a tool belt, like he's some damn authority. Professional? "Who you calling a professional?" I protest, let the "Negro" slide. "Let the Negro slide," Mr. Tool Belt says. OK, now I can't ignore that shit. Yes, the proverbial fan was involved, all hell was loosed, my spine still standing, everything else: a pile. The conductor announces Michigan St., four blocks past where I intended to exit. Somehow, I think he knows, but I have no proof other than my nerve. I ride the train. . .

How You Got Here

for Tamir

12 is the cinder: bright-
eyed boy w/pellet gun,
the coffin of plastic things,
        (draw & aim
        draw & aim).
Face immortalized
in perpetual smile, the soft
space a soccer ball lands. *Swear*
it was   an accident,
so boys say, same
ones crying
        That's the same thing you had on yesterday!
        What's wrong?
        Ya Momma ain't got no money?

How low we are,

                 target
2 seconds after cruiser
exit. Memory—
your insides escaping
through the hole
of a single slug. Ghost,
missing, black
helium rising,
angel wings fixed
to the back of your hoodie, ascension
on a random
city block.

        It is November.
                Cleveland is cold
as Cleveland often is.

The story is just that:
12-year-old you
falsely armed, the cops
falsely alarmed.

Continuum

After days of murder, more bodies
than nights in a week, you would think
we'd say *Enough*. Instead,
more blood. Don't think
it's just the dealers, that side
of law not in your nature.
It's expectant fathers on morning walks,
it's businessmen minding their business,
selling denim on Sunday afternoons.
Yesterday, my student, who doesn't believe
in gun control, said he wanted to write
a poem about parenting & the right
to bear arms, how slipping on one side
affects the other
(you guess
            which way that goes).
& though you won't find me w/steel
in the small of my back (@ least
not by my hand), I know the peace
a poem can bring. So I say, *Yes,
write*. & he goes back to his seat
nodding his head, the room filled
w/the voices of his classmates
comparing Dove, Simic, & Wright,
the push of my chair
back from my desk to stand & speak
like fingernails
on a chalk board, like a scream
when a gun   fires.

HOT

DO-NUTS

Long's Bakery

. . . .

Linda does a double take, says I remind her
of her brother.
                    This is what happens

to poets, conversations
out of the blue: the luxury
of a face

easy to talk to.
                I am sure there are secrets
in your hands, the careful measure

that picks two dozen yeast from the racks
to lay gently in a white waxed box,
a surprise for my students

on the last day of class, the sugar
before the bitter: midnight oil,
the As, the Fs, always a few

to deal, my hand growing lighter
w/no less swing.
& there is not a space to be had on this curb,

& the hunger in our bellies keeps us rushing the door,
& your kind eyes & hands keep searching
for soft places to sink our teeth.

Dismantle

You ring up my groceries & think it's OK
to tell the story of your brother, in anger,
calling his best friend gay. Not a story
of chastising your brother's intent, just a story
where gay is thrown about w/out conscience,
the awkward appendage.

        & what
        if I was?
The space between your eyebrows narrows, voice: a crack
& whine. Milk, beer & razors take a soldier's stance
in the rolling march of the belt. From the furrow & squeak,
I know offending me is the last thing on your mind.
        I am not here.
I am a cart of goods your hands rifle through hour after
hour, price check, total & nothingface you ask, "Paper
or plastic?" while thinking "When the hell can *I* leave?"
        All this
I want to say before you hand me the bags & I shuffle
into the whistling sting of evening. All these thoughts
for deaf ears. No. All these thoughts unspoken, the ear
never bent. What right have I to anger?

If There Is a Reason

Her fade tighter
than mine, the lines
some kind of resurrection.

                She bops,
earbuds in,
down an Indy street

in fall, the name,
no matter. She
is what gives the street

a reason. I am a lunchtime
drive-by, the dusty ride
that never catches her eye, mind

full of music. I can only
imagine her song by wire,
miles.

When a woman hits on you in a bookstore,

                    the world
comes together. Different
than supermarket browsing,
a lean & linger over a patch
of shriveling strawberries, the way
you took 10 minutes agonizing
over the freshest batch of kale
when your daily plate
is bread & potatoes. No,
these are conscious decisions,
mind taut & angular, a weapon
w/many edges. Not a dull cleaving
before the butcher's counter—
this   is serious.

& after the third time
she walks by the poetry aisle
where you laugh aloud about
[insert cool name here] she
approaches, basket brimming
w/Hurston, Baldwin, Larsen,
& a book of computer coding
you would pretend to understand
on any blessed night. "I was the one
from the parking lot, the one
who smiled when you walked in,"
she says,   & you
                    are alert. Alive.

Persist

II.
The door at 2 a.m.: a yawn
of wide silver mouth, our clutch

& unbuttoned clothes
exposed to gasps, the panic

of fingers in search of buttons
to seal us off again. Somehow,

in a gathering of thousands,
floor after floor, we never

reach a room.
Your smile, a promise, leads me

down loud carpet, a yellow mess
of crude angles, past one door, past

another, & out to the stairwell.
We shed clothes

as if they burn, declare
walls & rails are better

than beds, my arms heavy
w/your sweet weight, the curve

of your back falling into me . . .
. . . & the echo, louder, closer, one flight

& then the next—what moves
that is not our own.

Blood Houses

You are the segregated city no longer
mine, the din I drive through to get back
to now. I feel your eyes claw me
in coffee shops, the grocery, bookstores
that never sell my damn books, even though
Momma's water broke
& I raised my head from the Ohio.
This river is too shallow to sink my grief,

even my houses of blood—spread
East End to West End—make no nevermind.
I am a stranger here. & that boyhood
heart-in-throat cross of the Ohio
from IN to KY, the thrill of the wild
sprawling riverfront—slow fade.

You are the segregated city no longer
breathing. If poem-to-mouth resuscitation
could work, don't you think
I would have tried? My poems
cuss under their breath, say
I commit to too many voices, should be

committed. Sometimes, I am afraid
to listen.
        Let's say, for the sake of argument,
that what I write could revive you,
& I held a page to your lips, pinched
your nose, watched your chest

swell, your lungs fat
w/enjambment, volta, & you rose
from the floor in one fluid cough/cry,
liquids & sibilants whetting the angles
of your mouth . . . what then?
Would you beat down my door?

You are the segregated city no longer
willing. What choice, dear din,
have I?

127 Notebooks

for Nikky Finney

Back to your 14th year of living—
eagle eye, iambic breath—
127 spines numbered to the birth
of your recording, textual soundtrack.
I imagine you, Lynn Carol Finney,
light years more profound
than shortsight of the age allows,
how fallen leaves dance through your pages,
play possum for others. How
the carloads of books
your father bought, brought home,
were treasure, your lens growing
ever wider in the listening. Back to the sugar
of South Carolina sun, the way
the day boils & cools, leaves night
for the reckoning: the butterfly
you find dried on your windowsill,
wings as maps, traces of future
to follow. These precious echoes
wrapped between the covers, held
with both arms to your heart.
The things
you know,
girl. The poem
you will pick from journal #7
in the year of journal #17. The spines,
the spines. Back, back, sweet history,
the oddity & odd number
of 127, never awkward
in the ear's turntable.
How the story
always finds its way.

Amplified

(Iowa, Iowa, you have more poets than
              scarecrows these fuse-lit days).
   —*Rane Arroyo*

It gets tight sometimes. I
am learning my breath, how
deeply to inhale, when air
goes too far, presses lungs

to burst. But nothing moves
me like this. Headphones drown
out Iowa, the corn
fields waving heads

of silk across
the street, the family
who walks barefoot
in the snow, who stares through

us no matter the day. Daddy
would say we are equal, even
better, but something about our shades
didn't play—so there

was distance.
                 Iowa winters don't play
favorites, & I wonder
how their feet don't go

numb & submit to gravity,
send the boy, his momma
& daddy into the steely ice. I wonder
if he calls them

Momma & Daddy?
                 Another
album & I forget the people
downstairs who only talk

w/their eyes, my eyes
locked on a war
of colors, space-
ships, platform shoes,
& full-length furs. No church
like Kentucky; funk is my religion.
                    There are words my 7-year-old ears
shouldn't hear. I know this, I don't

say them, I just know, & what does
it matter w/the headphones on
& the needle searching the wax?
                    I can't tell you where Oakland is,

but I wish somebody would
take me. All I know is I want a voice
like Glenn's, one you get called on
to seep from your lips

in a whispered prayer, build
to the sky like each stone
in a pyramid. I want that sound
coming out of me, floating on a microphone,

amplified, a crowd glued to every note.

Swing down sweet
chariot, stop—

More snow will come today. Will
the family downstairs wear shoes?

Do they hear me sing along, in the quiet
of my bedroom, no other voice

but mine, calling into space. A signal
considered, a holy vessel contemplating

landing, burning circles
in the husk.

spark, earth

Abandon

1.21.2011
~~Lyrae Van Clief-Stefanon~~
For Debbie—
Joy! And
Blessings!
        —inscription in Open Interval

Debbie is not open to poetry, her friend
is mistaken. She takes
the gift with a smile, promises
to read every line her friend
suggests. *Andromeda, Ithaca,* good

so far. She is wrong; she does
like poetry. So does he. They meet
when Debbie opens *Interval*
at a campus coffee shop, the one
where the long lines

should warrant better brew. She nods,
feigns interest in his story
of an MFA, wanting to be
a professor, an author. It's nice
& all, but can't he see

she's reading? & anyway, who goes in
on career goals five minutes after
Hello? What would Lyrae say?
Sitting w/Matisse, unpacking flesh
& outline? Well, something

about him said Matisse, not the man,
the process, his fade & focus
like *Pink Nude*:
> abstract
> realist

> abstract
> realist
> before settling
on the weathered hip.
> What words

would a poet string
to spit shine soft pickup lines?
Debbie sinks
into the pages, leaves in such a spark
the book is abandoned. He attempts

to read the poems, wonders if
he can be an author after all, swears
he will give Debbie the book back
the next time he sees her,
sells it for cash instead.

Mother's Day

There is a Little League field near your house, the field
is full & it's Mother's Day. You are sure
that this is a comment on the failure
of patriarchy, but it's too late now. The team
in navy & scarlet is nothing special, at least
in terms of wardrobe, but the opposition:
flannel gray capped in white sleeves & gold script.
"Now they're just showing off," you think.
"That jersey is majestic."
& you mean it. Part of you
wouldn't be surprised to see
Satchel Paige swaying tall
@ the mound, or Josh Gibson
ready to knock the hide off the cork
@ the plate. These unis are playing
w/your mind. All this
you get
from two passes, your window
down, the stereo thumping
Hiatus Kaiyote, something
about fingerprints, Atari,
& lungs. & you could swear it's Iowa
City, the City Park baseball diamonds
all over again, your father,
an assistant coach, smiling as wide
as his Afro in the team pic, you
& he the only coffee beans
in the cream. You get
the dilemma, why father stays close,
encourages you to swing hard
for the tee & run. Run, son. Run
like you see another black boy
@ home plate & you are no longer
the lonely alone   passing through.

Farther

Today I boiled an egg
so long
it split

its skin
to free. I
smelled the yolk

& water burn,
but never rose
to see.

Love me again

in Hyde Park, feed me
salt carmel fudge, cups
of Johnny Drum. Catch
my eyes in the tight blue
booth, huddled over a two-
piece, salt & pepper

mild, Strawberry Crush. Wrap
your arms around my back, dig
the crates: *P-Funk
Earth Tour, Close
Encounters, Quiet
Fire.* Freeze

this day
like the grooves in the vinyl
I cart back to Indiana. Tell me
we'll return, warm
the booth
once more.

Persist

III.
Since she likes silence,
we lie in the wrap of after,
speaking with eyes, the graze
of wild fingers. She reaches
for the morning paper,
returns to my arms,
& the room is filled
w/rustling pages, the ring
of her smile. Still, no words
as another page turns, another
like us: face up, back
to earth.

&—in a Thousand-Yard Stare—Reverie

You look
> @ me
> as if
> I can
> define
> love. Good
> luck
> w/that.

-O

Your welcome
to the neighborhood
is the Crips killing a Dozen
Cousin 2 blocks down
from the townhouse
you just moved into, shot-
guns & shells
@ the community center
where you will take swimming lessons, sink
like a Midwest boy
out of time. This
after punk rock & bitter beer
in a church basement, bodies
slamming against each other as if dying
to be whole. This
after you are fresh
from cornfields, the silk
still in wisps
behind your ears.
          Years drift, & you curse
Columbus, wonder
Little Paul, Ray,
Stacy, Special K, the West
High good times crew.
                    Who is rotting
in the belly, who dared take
another bite, who
got past probation
officers visiting @ lunch time,
who endured the shaking
hand, the gat they had to grip
after school? Who can read
any of this, rise,
say *I*?

Monday morning, the first thing

from our mouths
is murder; in a phone call
to your mother's,
I spill news of Broad Ripple,
2 shot, 1 dead outside
a hookah lounge. You counter w/a knife
fight where you are, Louisville
matching Indy
blood for blood.
                    As if one story's
not enough, we pile our words
like corpses in open graves. Sorry,
too on the nose? How about one
hand stacked atop another, the closest
bones to God: victor. Something
about layers, something about
a winner & a loser, someone
on top & someone w/out air.

Your mother in the air
behind you tells me
Hello, the echo
shaking through
your cell, asks
for the *CJ* to browse
the obits for names
she knew in school.

Protocol

It's like when your uncle stops by, let's himself in,
& he's making small talk w/your Dad about how humid
it is, pay day & the Preakness, & he finally gets around
to asking your Dad where your Mom "his big sister"
is & Dad says, "Vegas," & you can swear the look on his face
says "Oh, I know what you want," & you try to wait
on your little brother to give him the baby shower gift
you missed from the night before, but he went back
to sleep, so you walk for the door, & if you're leaving,
you know uncle will follow, so you get ready for him
to ask for a ride home, but he asks for $20 for Pampers
& cigarettes—he could sell his food stamps tomorrow,
he says, but he needs the Pampers now—so you tell him
you don't have any cash (which is true) but you can drive
him to Kroger for Pampers & smokes, & you do, & he's not sure
if his daughter, your cousin, needs a size 3 or 4, 3 or 4 . . .
& he decides on 3, tucks the box under his arm, & walks
to checkout, asks for a hard pack of Marlboro reds, says he forgot
his phone or he would show you new pics of his daughter,
& you think he's talking to you, but he's talking to the cashier
who gets his smokes & smiles, places the hard pack on the counter
before you swipe your card. You drop him off on Market
across the street from a church still in session
after he throws the plastic from the hard pack out the window,
a dark blue Charger for 2 then 3 blocks closes in
on your bumper. "You know, I'll be 55 next month,"
he says. "You can drop me off here," midblock, not
at the house he's going to. You point your car east
for the rest of your drag through the old neighborhood
until you find the on-ramp, turn left on 65. & dammit,
by now you should know
that this is not a poem, not
a poem at all. By now,
it's a knee & the dirt
that keeps it wet.

Persist

IV.
In the dream, I lead you
to a place of mirrors, our hearts
reflecting on themselves. We glow
in candlelight, now halos

in the mirror's bend. There is no sound
but our breath, the mirrors fogged, nothing
more to say.   Tell me
what you hear.

{Ení Dreams (w/Regrets)}

Even death
seemed different to him—a place where she
would be waiting
        —Sharon Olds

In the dream, She is two: the one
in bed & the one @ the window. Before
bed, you pull back the curtains,
find her standing outside, a smile,
a hand on the glass. You add yours,
feel warmth between the pane. Finally,
bed. You are lying
face to face, clear as day (Why
doesn't she hold you anymore?)
when you feel a body slip
beneath the cover, wrap
its arms around your back.
It is she of the window, same
face as the lover in your bed,
except her body doesn't fear
yours, & she is ready to love
you fully. But what about the other,
she disrupts your touch
w/the other her, says that part
of her is missing like
your love, & maybe you
should call it quits. & you
agree until you realize
her version of quit calls for you
deceased, & she reaches
for a knife, looks for places to land
the blade in the dark. & why
can't you just wake up
like normal people, say
I can't remember
my dreams.

Montgomery

When night falls
& stories turn on themselves,
twist into
the undoing, a stranger

@ the hipster bar asks
"Where you from?"
You respond, "Kentucky,"
& he with four drinks

sloshing liquor on your table
tells you he'll be "politically correct"
when he recalls the story
of a black guy

who pulled a gun
& found a place
to rest the barrel
@ his temple.

Sugar Hill

"It looks like everything to do with you has a hex on it."
—Fabulous to his man, Morgan

Langston is dead. There is no poetry @ Club Haiti.
Greed beat a man for a dollar, patent leather zip boot kick to rib cage,
full moon pummel, cowards fleeing the scene like end rhyme. Boss man
Morgan (what kind of name is that for a gangster?) leaves him a face down
snow angel in parking lot gravel, like Sugar never loved him—like the living
can't plot revenge. Enter the undead w/the help of Mama Maitresse (yes,
that's Mother Jefferson, but this poem ain't about a deeelux apartment.
Pay attention). Morgan's fatal mistake met w/payback: a beheading w/slave
shackle evidence, offal as pig swill. When the thugs realize bullets don't
stop zombies, machetes match their fear, & Sugar is caesura. Something
you should know: When a woman is willing to sell her soul to avenge her
lover's death, there is no such thing as daylight if you are the greed in
her way.

Caterwaul

I awake w/two
wishbones in my mouth,
a sun so bright
what good are eyes?
No shortage of wishes,
I remove the bones
one by one, compare the bend
& curve, which
might snap
first.
        What shall I dream?
I live w/the fear
that my days are short, snuffed
by means outside my body.
I used to wonder what the day
would be like, when you finally know
if there's another side, somewhere else
bright & singing after all this,
& you know
but can't tell a soul.

Family Business: Indy

Give it to them: Dinner was OK—
not outstanding, OK. The pepper
& sugar of the General Tso's
was not the homemade fresh
you had here before new management
took the weight, but you put that aside
(& damn that Netflix doc; this is real
food to you).
              Tonight, your 8-year-old
is a big girl, holds the menu
arms wide, makes her own
choices for what she'll eat—
shrimp fried rice & vegtable eggroll—
eyes glazed w/lines
of Chinese characters built
like tiny houses, the coil
of dragons, the print
in bold, bold red.
              You watch
the door. Because
it is a slow night
& you are the only patrons,
& you know this guncentric city.

Across the parking lot sits the gas station
where the high school kids
walked in armed, where @ least
one clerk never came home
from the night shift, the last
bit of light through the slit of their eyes
the faces of children
wrapped in bandannas,
apparitions w/out the bough.
& you wonder how anyone works
in the constant threat
of chaos, how you blank out

the risk of gun & theft
for the next check. How
is this living? How do you keep
your daughter's mind on the feast
before her, not the threat
@ her back?

Clip

Bullets ain't racial kid, they only hate you.
    —Kool G. Rap

No.
        The magazines considered here have nothing to do
w/ways to keep your man wanting more; 10 diet tips to lose
10 pounds by summer, recipes involving tuna, cheese &/or
mystery meat your family won't eat. When 16's in the clip
& one's in the chamber, every body will have pounds
to lose.
        Summertime, and the living
ain't living, hair-trigger finger, sweat
in the way of right.
                        Remember summer '06, two years
before the baby, fresh out of grad school,
the move to Indy & the inexplicable
body count? Was that summer or greed
w/out season, flatline & kiss
of scythe? When death comes so often,
who can heal?
        We plant roots in this place,
survive a diet
of its pain. She is our Circle, wounded,
w/child, some wandering, some
streets w/out light, some waiting
to be born, make a way
through the bullet & haze.
& I would be less than honest
if I didn't hold your hand
in the bed where our daughter was made,
say that adding another heart
to this house
has me thinking of a night
when the latch is off the door
& a heavy boot sends the plank on a fall,
& we find ourselves in the kitchen @ zero
hour & fight whatever is staring back
in the uneasy dark. & that something

staring back ain't kicking
in doors & knuckling up.
They'll have steel,
& what if I want more
than hands?

Haints

The people of the Future
drink the moon
Everything is possible
    —Mari Evans

Maybe Bobby gets too much credit.

                    Maybe that night
when his voice bounced against
the Naptown dark
& his uneasy sigh
loosed the letters that spelled kin's death,
God's rain spit the echoes of haints
against his face & his obituary
cooled in night's breath, brushed
shoulders w/the crowd's synced scream.

Dearest reader, take no offense,
this is not to suggest the act
was not shouting down a bullet,
that Bobby didn't wish peace. Honestly,
I am an errant kite ensnared in limbs
knowing his eyes would never open
in another 2 months, that he knew the price
for free speech was death,
talked anyway.

Maybe the Circle never fired because the crowd remembered
Emmett
& Medgar
& Addie Mae
& Denise
& Cynthia
& Carole
& Johnny
& Virgil

& JFK
& James
& Andrew
& Michael

    & Malcolm
    & Malcolm
    & Malcolm.

Maybe black folks said
Everything is burned inside me;
I am no friend of bomb or flame,
& when I wake in the morning,
I want to see the corner store
clean & whole
like it was before my sleep.

because he is a bloody pulp,
the losing end of a back alley
beat down, attempt @ justice
shot to hell. A hot New York
blackout, summer '77,
the hookers & pimps
ruling the square, a vigilante
types a new entry in his journal
about washing, cleansing, righting
the earth, his own blood
in the margins. & you, faithful
reader, practically panting
between the "hero's" hot-
plate favors & momentary
clean-diner peace before another
splintered door, another
kick to fracture limb, pretend
this isn't why you read him—
poor bag man—like you don't love
rooting for a rube w/less
of a shot than you, like you
have some answers
for stopping blood.

Is it wrong

that I ignore the Witness @ my door, turn back
to the kitchen, pour

another cup of coffee, whisper
Mercy?   I know

what you'll say, no different
than the last ring, arms

full of *Watchtower*s, a Bible, always
in twos—some kind

of safety.
            I can't

            blame you,
but if we aren't talking

about bullets, I don't
want to ponder

salvation. I don't want
to ignore Altons & Philandos

& how
on earth

did they get those marquee names?
Were their mothers

seers, did they know
their sons

would be footnotes, #s? If
I answer the doorbell that cuts

& drums the hollow
of this house, the blood

you raise in conversation
will not be Sandra's or Rekia's,

& what's the use, I think. Don't ask
me about a kingdom,

don't ask
if I've been saved.

Persist

V.
If I could work the kink out of my tongue, love,
I would say you are no small thing to lose,
the prayer that clasps hands in small hours,
Moleskine scratch, pearl of sweat. We

are young, time our rosary,
& so good @ wasting time, so good
@ wasting. On a night w/no moon,
faint breeze, the eternal optimist

dubbed memory, I dream the kisses
never planted, your face in my hands, arms
around my waist, sweet vines, calling
Closer, love.   Closer   still.

When You Know, Logically, That Death Is Not Just a
Matter of Rest but a Way of Making Space For New
People On Earth, &, Quite Honestly, After All You've
Loved, Pampered & Lost, You, Selfish By Your Own
Admission, Could Care Less

Who sat   eyes
shut—waited
for more?   The title,
dammit . . .

Tout De Suite

After finding the receipt
for the overpriced burger you
devoured in that hipster bar
in the new up-&-coming (i.e.
gentrified) part of town, you
don't wince. You don't curse
yourself for the black
& white proof of overindulgence
staring back @ you. No, none
of that. Instead, you remember
the sweet of the grind, the heft
in your hand, bubble & pop
of the pint that washed it down (another
dollar waste). Remember,
it was escape, silent & alone, you ate
every morsel, even the crumbs
of beef & bread that fell back
to the plate. What kind
of world is this? You wanted
to ask, kept picking
until the plate was bare.
Like you. Now.

on the Wife's Return, the Lovers Kiss the Airport

Swear
I can hear
lips smacking.

Her crane-neck peer into tinted
windows, his surprise that his love
is just outside. The dance around
the car, wide grin, awkward reach
to have her in his arms, her arms
still suitcase-full. Then the smack
of lips above the warm stir
of evening. Over & over
& over. But I think love
should have music; what's wrong
w/that? & what's wrong—
in a throng of strangers—
about grabbing your heart's desire
& wetting lips on a waiting curb?
I'm serious, what's wrong
w/that? This is not
a rhetorical question. & another
thing: I think we cheat ourselves
calling this PDA, emotional
shorthand for the act
we all desire. Stop
being lazy, open
your eyes.

Call it what it is.

Workers, Morning: The Thirsty Scholar

Every other word is
"fucking." The workers
ask for a breakfast spot
when bagels & quiche &
scones are already on the menu,
the implication: That's not
breakast, or "That's not fucking
breakfast," as the dirtied
worker would say, filthy
by his own admission.
I wonder
what O'Hara would feed
their torsos, what sweat
& heat he would have seep
from the wounds
their mouths make.
I like that I walk
into this place, drop
the temperature
of the room,
make necks twist
to understand my hoodie & Js
clashing w/wood & wrought
iron, marble table
tops, white. "You talk
so much shit . . . "
"It took you a fucking
hour . . . "
the dirtied worker's
voice trails off into another
chain of expletives.
"Yeah, we are," rings out
as the warble & jangle
of the band X stops suddenly.
The night-haired waitress
w/her locks wrapped to bun

takes my plate
w/out words, taps the tile
to the next table to chirp
something to a patron
out of earshot. There is no
reason for me to come
back, no morsel left
to feed my curiosity, but
I do understand,
in the profane & silent,
the ornaments
of privilege,
your discomfort—
how none are spared
the taste.

{Ení (of the Unreliable Knuckles)}

Laugh if you want (promise
me you won't), but the first
thing that comes to mind
in these hard hours is a good
fist fight. I can't fight
for shit, born on the same
streets Ali beed & butterflied,
& I would likely break my hand
w/a punch before any bone
in your body, but this is what
I want—fists trembling, pace
& shuffle, honest sweat, trash talk
& outright threats. It doesn't matter
if I lose, if I can't tell the difference
between my teeth & the gravel
that balances my knees. What matters
is that I swing & swing
w/intent, that I hurl my hand
w/the mind to bruise.

Confession:

I have not written a poem
in months, but I love you. That
is poem enough. If I count
the days of silence, render
my debt in absent ear,

a broken heart
makes no poem. It is
the mending, love, the way
we bind the pieces
whole. The body

fluid, singular—day-
dream, learning how
to feel, float. That
is poem & love,
the angles, breaks.

Prosody

after Yusef Komunyakaa

No one in the house speaks
to me. I hold two
fingers to my neck
("Better safe," we say).

The iambs
in my chest are slower
than yesterday, like
the drummer senses heart
break, tosses the rim-
shot for brushes: rasp
& sweep. I walk
for the door, say goodbye,
but no one answers. The seats
of my car are still warm
like someone has been driving
w/out me. In my side view mirror,

       the woman
in the car behind
cries, or is that singing?
       Or maybe, she
is brushing a lash
from her eye, the dark
quill falling into her lap. & all
I have is want, neither
salt nor wet.

A grandmother asks me how to spell divine

& I get it wrong.
               Look, she says,
I know you are busy, your hands
filled with copies, but is this
right? She holds out a handmade card
for her granddaughter, "You are everything,"
the card declares, "& my love for you
is eternal, devine."
D-e-v-i-n-e. Yes, that's right,
I reply, gather my copies
& rush to my car. *D-e-*
v-i-n-e. D-e-v-i—no.
               I wave my arms from the seat
of my car, hope to catch her eye,
rush back though the door to admit we
are wrong. Who could live
w/that guilt, the perfect keepsake
stained? Who could drive away?

Jack London Square, September

Looking at his statue, a couple
debates whether London was a poet
or an author, poet or an author . . . the words
milling out of their puzzled mouths to float
on the breeze off the Bay. Three more nights
in Oakland before I am back on a plane to middle
America w/questions of my own. The plaque
@ London's feet is a quote from the man, something
about how he won't waste his days, how
his feet will bear canyons, how he
will burn the hours from the inside out. Perhaps
some of that is my own embellishment,
perhaps it's my desire.

                         A businessman shuffles
the water's cobblestone border, his ear
pressed to a cell, index finger
marking air, a notepad & pen
atop a nearby bench, black leather
briefcase open, stealing sun. Why
must he take so much
space? He
who looks back @ me once, twice—
like who is this six feet & scruff
taking in the water, spying me. As if
a poet would care
about his business, want
like he wants.

Tongues

What if you'd settled & stayed in your place
among friends who'd never arrive at that fork
in the road of their flat Midwestern lives
            —Al Young

Figure I'm halfway done, the poems
cursing beneath their breath, a good time
to trade coasts. Not a visit, I mean
until the end. I have fallen
for the Bay, can see a new life bound

to water. I would rent a modest apartment,
preferably above a bookstore. In the ideal
scenario, the super
owns the shop & gives me a discount
(on books, not rent. That would be

fantasy). The neighborhood is full
of restaurants: Mexican, Italian,
Indian. I've never been a cook,
but have no fear of honest work.
I could wash dishes, mop the kitchen

when the eyes cool. The chef
sees that I take pride in small things,
knows that I know the details matter.
Maybe he sees that & says, *Tell you what,*
we'll start w/salads & see

where things go. Deal?
I turn radish to rose, wedge
tomatoes, rinse endive & spinach,
pat the greens dry.
& the chef knows

I mean business,
& he, a man of his word,
moves the new dishwasher up,
puts a sauté pan in my hand
& says, *Hermano. Cook.*

      On my off days,
I never fire an eye, figure
that's work. I sip morning coffee
@ the bookstore, thumb a copy
of *Kaddish,* imagine the cost
of losing a mother, the mind
before the body. My poems
stand in line @ the register, cut

their eyes, say *Poeta: You
have abandoned us.*   I pretend
not to hear.   The book
back on the shelf, I comb the blocks

before me, browse menus
in windows, read
FRIED PIGEON.   Stop.

       Read it again.
Wings beat against my lips,

shoppers pass, rush
to nearby markets,

stuff paper bags w/onions,
carrots, bok choy. Two men

haggle over the price
of dried peppers . . .

. . . FRIED PIGEON . . .
A boy on the corner

raises a pinwheel
to the afternoon breeze . . .

& writing poems?
What of it?

Epilogue

Laugh if you want (promise
your spine exposed

me. You won't), but the first
night after night

thing that comes to mind
standing in place

in these hard hours is a good
here, & what's that like,

fist fight? I can't fight
is not your home, but you are

FOR shit, born on the same
to say *This:*

streets Ali beed & butterflied,
There is no other way,

& I would likely break my hand
enough to keep

w/a punch before any bone
of value, but not

in your body. But this is what
were thought to be something—

There is no easy way to explain this,
for this or that, tercet & foot, & you

I want—fists-trembling pace.
There was a question of worth, how much,

& shuffle, honest sweat, trash talk
(Or)

& outright threats. It doesn't matter
w/out, plot & POV, & you

if I lose, if I can't tell the difference,
thought about what they could do

between my teeth & the gravel
w/little space for extra, someone

that balances my knees. What matters
(Or)

is that I swing & swing
here

w/intent, that I hurl my hand
w(h)ere unwanted & you wound up

w/the mind to bruise.
But there was a time when you—

{Ení (of the unreliable knuckles)}—
Used. Sold.